BUILD A BETTER LIFE
BY STEALING OFFICE S

DOGBERT'S BIG BOOK OF BUSINESS

illustrated by
SCOTT ADAMS

SUPPLIES

nb
NICHOLAS BREALEY
PUBLISHING
LONDON

For the twentieth of every month

First published in Great Britain
by Nicholas Brealey Publishing Ltd in 1992
36 John Street
London WC1N 2AT

Reprinted 1992, 1994 (twice), 1996, 1997 (twice), 1998

ISBN 185788 0153

First published in USA by Topper Books
an imprint of Pharos Books in 1991

British Library Cataloguing in Publication Data
A catalogue record for this book is available
from the British Library.

Printed in Finland by Werner Söderström Oy

Dogbert and Dilbert appear regularly in their own comic strip, Dilbert® featured in *Today*

BUILD A BETTER LIFE
BY STEALING OFFICE SUPPLIES
CONTENTS

FOREWORD by Dogbert

Many pompous business books have been written in the last few years. This is another one. But unlike its predecessors, this book offers practical information.

Other business books have offered such useful insights as "profitable companies pay high salaries." What exactly are we supposed to do with that kind of information? Should unprofitable companies raise salaries to become more profitable?

Let's face it, companies that are profitable are usually in the right place at the right time, and that's all there is to it. Those companies could be managed by gerbils and they would still make money hand over paw. Sure, in the beginning somebody invented something valuable, or stole it from somebody else, but since then it's been strictly auto-pilot.

So forget about making the company more profitable; it's out of your control. Put your energy where it will make the most difference: surviving your frustrating and thankless job.

What the world needs is a practical guide to business——one which the average white collar worker can understand and use. That's why I wrote **Dogbert's Big Book of Business**. That's why it has simple cartoon pictures.

To research this book I spent nearly two weeks working at a large American company. This was long enough to become an expert by American standards, but not so long that the life force would be sucked out of me.

I hope you enjoy my book.

DRESSING FOR SUCCESS

MEN'S BUSINESS CLOTHES

A MAN'S BUSINESS CLOTHES ARE THE MOST IMPORTANT DETERMINANT OF HOW HE IS TREATED.

THESE CLOTHES SAY "I WILL BE A GRUMPY CLERK FOREVER. TREAT ME LIKE EAR WAX."

THESE CLOTHES SAY "I AM BOUND FOR MANAGEMENT. PRETEND YOU LIKE ME BECAUSE I COULD BE YOUR BOSS SOMEDAY."

THESE CLOTHES SAY "I'M THE ONLY ONE WHO UNDERSTANDS THE COMPUTER SYSTEM. WORSHIP ME."

S.Adams

WOMEN'S BUSINESS CLOTHES

WOMEN UNDERSTAND HOW TO USE BUSINESS CLOTHES TO CONVEY SUBTLE MESSAGES.

THESE CLOTHES SAY "I LIKE EATING CHOCOLATE MORE THAN I LIKE THIS STUPID JOB."

THESE CLOTHES SAY "I AM A SUCCESSFUL BUSINESS WOMAN. GET OUT OF MY WAY, DAMN IT."

THESE CLOTHES SAY "I HOPE YOU WILL IGNORE THE STUFF THAT COMES OUT OF MY MOUTH."

S. Adams

STAINS

YOUR BUSINESS CLOTHES ARE NATURALLY ATTRACTED TO STAINING LIQUIDS. THE ATTRACTION IS STRONGEST JUST BEFORE AN IMPORTANT MEETING.

COFFEE

TIME FOR MY MEETING.

S. Adams

BUSINESS ETIQUETTE

THE POWER HANDSHAKE

YOU CAN GAIN IMMEDIATE
DOMINANCE IN A BUSINESS
SITUATION BY FORCING
THE OTHER PERSON TO
SHAKE HANDS LIKE A
PATHETIC WIMP.

APPROACH
NORMALLY

CLAMP THEIR
FINGERTIPS

SHAKE THEIR
HELPLESS HAND
LIKE A DEAD
SPARROW

HALLWAY ETIQUETTE

THE ACCEPTED RULES OF
HALLWAY ETIQUETTE COVER
ONLY THE FIRST TWO TIMES
YOU RUN INTO THE SAME
PERSON IN THE SAME DAY.
AFTER THAT, YOU MUST
IMPROVISE.

SALARY ETIQUETTE

IT IS CONSIDERED IMPOLITE TO ASK
CO-WORKERS THEIR SALARIES; HOWEVER,
IT IS PERFECTLY ACCEPTABLE TO DEDUCE
IT BY GRILLING THEM RELENTLESSLY ON
THEIR SPENDING HABITS.

DOGBERT'S LEISURE PERCEPTION PRINCIPLE

WHEN PEOPLE ARE NOT BUSY, THEY BELIEVE THAT YOU ARE ALSO NOT BUSY. YOUR SUBTLE HINTS TO THE CONTRARY WILL NOT BE EFFECTIVE. SOMETIMES IT WILL BE NECESSARY TO FAKE YOUR OWN DEATH.

THE DOGBERT HARP

IF SOMEBODY MISSPEAKS AT A MEETING, IT IS YOUR OBLIGATION TO HARP ON IT OVER AND OVER AGAIN.

...AND GROSS SALES ARE DOWN TEN PERCENT THIS MONTH.

YOU MEAN YEAR, NOT MONTH.

TEN PERCENT THIS MONTH ?!! IT'S IMPOSSIBLE. YOU HAVE LOST ALL CREDIBILITY. HOW CAN WE TRUST ANYTHING YOU SAY ?!!

I MEANT "YEAR"... I MISSPOKE.

TEN PERCENT A MONTH ?!! DO YOU TAKE US FOR IDIOTS ?!!

PERSONAL PHONE CALLS

IF YOU HAVE A PERSONAL LIFE, LET EVERYBODY ENJOY IT. SIGNAL YOUR CO-WORKERS TO LISTEN TO YOUR PERSONAL CALLS BY CHANGING YOUR POSTURE AND LOWERING YOUR VOICE.

OFFICE POLITICS

DEMAGOGUERY

ONE SURE WAY TO THE TOP IS TO INVENT SCAPEGOATS IN THE COMPANY AND LEAD THE CHARGE AGAINST THEM. IDEALLY, THE SCAPEGOATS SHOULD BE POWERLESS AND FUNNY LOOKING.

I HAVE TRACED THE SOURCE OF OUR DECLINING MARKET SHARE TO WILLY, OUR MAIL DELIVERY BOY.

WILLY MUST BE ELIMINATED, AND I MUST BE PROMOTED FOR SOLVING THE PROBLEM.

← DEATH

DOGBERT'S LAUGHTER GUIDE

THE AMOUNT OF ENERGY SPENT LAUGHING AT A JOKE SHOULD BE DIRECTLY PROPORTIONAL TO THE HIERARCHICAL STATUS OF THE JOKE TELLER.

LAUGHING AT YOUR BOSS'S JOKE

HEE HEE! I'LL HAVE TO REMEMBER THAT.

YOUR BOSS'S BOSS'S JOKE.

HA HA HA !! I'LL HAVE TO WRITE THAT ONE DOWN.

YOUR BOSS'S BOSS'S BOSS'S JOKE

HA HA HA
I'LL HAVE TO TATTOO THAT ON MY BACK !!!

STAYING OUT OF TROUBLE

OFFICE POLITICS

YOUR BOSS REACHED HIS/HER POSITION BY BEING POLITIC- ALLY ASTUTE. DON'T TURN YOUR BACK.

TWO SCOOPS OF...

ERK...

AM I NEXT?

TAKING CREDIT FOR OTHER PEOPLE'S WORK

IT IS MUCH EASIER TO TAKE CREDIT FOR OTHER PEOPLE'S WORK THAN TO DO YOUR OWN. GRAB EVERY OPPORTUNITY TO ASSOCIATE YOURSELF WITH PROJECTS WHICH ARE ALREADY SUCCESSFUL.

DE-POLITICIZING YOUR BUSINESS WRITING

BE CAREFUL THAT WHAT YOU WRITE DOES NOT OFFEND ANYBODY OR CAUSE PROBLEMS WITHIN THE COMPANY. THE SAFEST APPROACH IS TO REMOVE ALL USEFUL INFORMATION.

TAKE OUT THE DISCUSSION OF THE PROBLEM; IT COULD EMBARRASS SOMEBODY.

AND DON'T MENTION THE ALTERNATIVES; IT WILL JUST RAISE QUESTIONS.

OKAY, WHAT'S LEFT?

THE PAGE NUMBERS.

INEFFICIENCY AND YOUR CAREER

YOUR CAREER DEPENDS ON HOW MANY
PEOPLE WORK UNDER YOU. IT IS IN
YOUR BEST INTEREST TO INVOLVE AS
MANY PEOPLE AS POSSIBLE IN ANY
TASK. THAT WAY YOU CAN JUSTIFY
INCREASING YOUR STAFF.

IF YOU HAVE NO SPECIAL
TALENTS, AN UNGLAMOROUS
METHOD IS AVAILABLE TO
DISTINGUISH YOURSELF IN
YOUR BOSS'S EYES.

CHANGE FOR THE SAKE OF PROMOTION

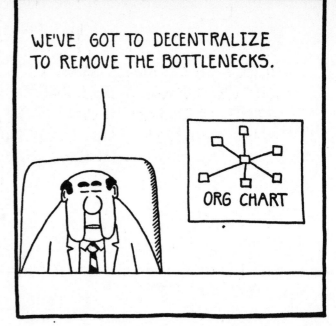

INSENSITIVITY: YOUR KEY TO MANAGEMENT SUCCESS

MONEY

CHANGES TO THE SALARY PLAN

ANY CHANGE TO THE SALARY PLAN WILL
RESULT IN LESS MONEY FOR YOU. IF
THEY WANTED TO GIVE YOU <u>MORE</u> MONEY,
THEY WOULDN'T HAVE TO GO THROUGH
ALL THE TROUBLE OF CHANGING THE PLAN.

THIS YEAR, ALL
RAISES WILL BE
ROUNDED TO THE
NEAREST TEN
PERCENT.

YOURS ROUNDS
DOWN TO ZERO.

YOUR SALARY

WHAT MOTIVATES MANAGERS

COMPANIES WITH NO MEANINGFUL MANAGEMENT INCENTIVES OF THEIR OWN END UP BEING MANAGED BY AIRLINE BONUS MILES PROGRAMS.

MONEY AS A MOTIVATOR...

HERE'S YOUR RAISE.

POINK

PRIDE AS A MOTIVATOR...

HERE ARE YOUR NEW BUSINESS CARDS. THEY SPELLED YOUR NAME WRONG BUT I FIGURED IT DIDN'T MATTER.

BONUS MILES AS A MOTIVATOR...

THE STAFF MEETING WILL BE IN AUSTRIA THIS WEEK!

I'LL BE THERE!

S.Adams

FANTASY BUDGETING

NEVER BASE YOUR BUDGET REQUESTS ON REALISTIC ASSUMPTIONS, AS THIS COULD LEAD TO A DECREASE IN YOUR FUNDING.

PLANNING YOUR BUDGET

THERE IS NO RELATIONSHIP BETWEEN YOUR ASSESSMENT OF YOUR BUDGET NEEDS AND WHAT YOU ACTUALLY RECEIVE.

HOW YOU CALCULATE IT

PERFECT... IT TOOK MONTHS, BUT I'VE DOCUMENTED MY BUDGET NEEDS DOWN TO THE DETAIL OF EVERY PENCIL.

HOW YOU GET IT

TAKE LAST YEAR'S BUDGET AND SUBTRACT TEN PERCENT.

THE GOOD MANAGEMENT PENALTY

MANAGEMENT SALARY INCENTIVES

MANAGEMENT SALARY INCENTIVES ARE DESIGNED TO EVENTUALLY ELIMINATE ALL EMPLOYEES.

I COULD GIVE YOU A BIG RAISE...

OR I COULD FIRE YOU, EARN A BIG BONUS FOR CUTTING EXPENSES, AND MAKE THE OTHERS IN YOUR GROUP WORK HARDER...

DECISIONS, DECISIONS...

THE BUREAUCRACY

GROUP WRITING

FEW THINGS IN LIFE ARE LESS EFFICIENT THAN A A GROUP OF PEOPLE TRYING TO WRITE A SENTENCE. THE ADVANTAGE OF THIS METHOD IS THAT YOU END UP WITH SOMETHING FOR WHICH YOU WILL NOT BE PERSONALLY BLAMED.

DOGBERT'S THEORY OF EMPLOYEE SUGGESTIONS

EMPLOYEE SUGGESTIONS ARE ALWAYS EVALUATED BY THE PERSON WHO SHOULD HAVE THOUGHT OF THE IDEA IN THE FIRST PLACE.

WILL I GET A CASH AWARD FOR MY EMPLOYEE SUGGESTION?

WELL, GEE, YOUR SUGGESTION MAKES ME LOOK STUPID BECAUSE YOU'RE TELLING ME HOW TO DO MY JOB.

S.Adams

SADLY, YOU ARE NOT ELIGIBLE FOR A CASH AWARD BECAUSE I THOUGHT OF THIS EXACT IDEA AN HOUR AGO.

KNOWING THE ENEMY

BEFORE YOU CAN DEFEAT THE COMPETITION, FIRST YOU MUST DEFEAT YOUR OWN COMPANY.

THIS IS THE PROJECT PLAN...

WE'LL IGNORE OUR LEGAL DEPARTMENT...

BYPASS THE ACCOUNTING DEPARTMENT...

INSTIGATE A FIGHT BETWEEN MARKETING AND OPERATIONS...

AND PRAY NOBODY NOTICES OUR PROJECT.

THE DOGBERT PHONE METHOD

FOLLOW THESE STEPS
TO GET RID OF CALLERS
WHO WANT INFORMATION.

1. NO MATTER WHAT THEY ASK, JUST GIVE THEM THE INFORMATION YOU HAVE RIGHT IN FRONT OF YOU.

I'VE GOT SOME GOOD INFORMATION ON THE DAYS OF THE WEEK . . .

2. IF THE CALLER PROTESTS, MAKE THEM RESTATE THE QUESTION. IN AS MANY FORMS AS POSSIBLE.

HOW WOULD THE HOPI INDIANS PHRASE THAT?

S.Adams

3. ACT LIKE THE CALLER'S QUESTION MAKES NO SENSE WHATSOEVER.

ARE YOU TALKING PIG LATIN? WHAT DO ALL OF THOSE WORDS MEAN?

CONTINUED...

4. PAUSE TWENTY SECONDS AND PRETEND YOU'VE FORGOTTEN THE ENTIRE CONVERSATION.

HELLO, HAVE YOU BEEN HELPED?

5. NOW PUT THE CALLER ON HOLD AND DISCONNECT AFTER TEN MINUTES.

OOPS!

6. IF THEY CALL BACK, SCAN THE OBITUARIES AND REFER THE CALLER TO THE RECENTLY DECEASED.

BOY, I HOPE NOTHING EVER HAPPENS TO OL'... BEN... BECAUSE HE'S THE ONLY ONE WHO CAN ANSWER YOUR QUESTION.

J. Adams

7. IF THE PEST CALLS YOU AGAIN, SLIP INTO A FOREIGN ACCENT AND START OVER AT STEP ONE.

YA, VEE GOT ZUM DAYS OF ZE VEEK RIGHT HERE, BY YIMMINY!

THE DOGBERT SHUFFLE

YOUR PERCEIVED VALUE TO THE COMPANY IS DIRECTLY RELATED TO THE VOLUME OF PAPER YOU SHUFFLE. REQUEST COPIES OF ALL DOCUMENTS, NO MATTER HOW UNRELATED TO YOUR RESPONSIBILITIES.

DID YOU READ THE NEWSPAPER TODAY?

NO. CAN YOU MAKE A COPY FOR ME?

DO YOU WANT A COPY OF MY REPORT ON THE MEDICAL BENEFITS OF WAVING YOUR ARMS AROUND?

BETTER GIVE ME TWO — I'M DOUBLE-JOINTED.

YOU MIGHT NEED TO LOOK UP SOME OF THE MEDICAL TERMS IN THE DICTIONARY.

MAYBE YOU COULD RUN OFF A FEW COPIES OF THE DICTIONARY TOO.

DOGBERT'S PROJECT PLANNING FORMULA

THE TIME TO COMPLETE ANY PROJECT CAN BE ESTIMATED BY MULTIPLYING THE NUMBER OF PEOPLE INVOLVED BY ONE WEEK.

MAKING EXCEPTIONS

DOGBERT'S LAW OF BUREAUCRATIC GRIDLOCK

BUREAUCRATIC GRIDLOCK IS CAUSED BY PEOPLE WITH DIFFERENT PRIORITIES WHO PRACTICE GOOD TIME MANAGEMENT.

DID YOU GET THE INFORMATION I NEED FOR MY IMPORTANT PROJECT?

NO. IT'S NOT IN MY TOP THOUSAND PRIORITIES.

DID YOU BRING THE INFORMATION I REQUESTED FOR MY IMPORTANT PROJECT.

NO, BECAUSE YOUR PROJECT DOESN'T MATTER TO ME.

THOSE TIME MANAGEMENT CLASSES SURE HAVE FREED UP OUR SCHEDULES.

THE ANSWER DEPENDS ON THE ASKER

NEVER ANSWER A QUESTION UNLESS YOU KNOW EXACTLY WHO IS ASKING, WHY IT IS BEING ASKED, AND WHAT WILL BE DONE WITH THE INFORMATION.

CAN I ASK YOU A QUESTION?

WHY DO YOU WANT TO KNOW? WHAT GROUP ARE YOU WITH? HOW WILL YOU USE THIS INFORMATION? ARE YOU GOING TO QUOTE ME? WHO ELSE ARE YOU TALKING TO? WHAT'S YOUR REAL MOTIVE HERE?

ACTUALLY, I JUST WANT DIRECTIONS TO THE MEN'S ROOM.

FOR YOUR OWN USE?

THE ADVANTAGE OF SMALL COMPANIES

BIG COMPANIES USE MOST OF THEIR RESOURCES TRYING TO KEEP PEOPLE FROM GETTING MAD AT THEM. SMALL COMPANIES HAVE MORE FLEXIBILITY.

MANAGEMENT BY SHAKING THE BOX

THE BENEFITS OF TITLE INFLATION

INFLATED JOB TITLES IN MIDDLE MANAGEMENT ALLOW THOSE AT THE BOTTOM OF THE COMPANY HIERARCHY TO AVOID TRULY DEMEANING TITLES.

VICE PRESIDENT

ASSISTANT VICE PRESIDENT

EXECUTIVE MANAGER

MANAGER

PEON

ASSISTANT PEON

TEMP

BOOT-LICKING, LOWER-THAN-DIRT, ASSISTANT PEON.

S.Adams

PERFORMANCE AND PRODUCTIVITY

COFFEE PERFORMANCE GUIDE

YOUR HAPPINESS AND JOB
PERFORMANCE ARE INFLU-
ENCED MORE BY COFFEE
THAN BY ANY OTHER FACTOR.

NO COFFEE

ONE CUP   TWO CUPS   THREE CUPS   FOUR CUPS

DOGBERT'S THEORY OF MONDAYS

DOGBERT'S THEORY OF PERFORMANCE PERSPECTIVES

YOU AND YOUR BOSS WILL HAVE A DIFFERENT PERSPECTIVE ON YOUR PERFORMANCE.

CUBICLES

YOUR BOSS

LAW OF PROXIMITY

THE NEARER YOU ARE TO YOUR
BOSS'S OFFICE, THE LOWER THE
QUALITY OF YOUR ASSIGNMENTS.

BASIC MANAGEMENT TYPES

ALL MANAGERS FALL INTO ONE OF SEVERAL CATEGORIES. THE BEST YOU CAN HOPE IS TO HAVE A BOSS WHO DOESN'T NAUSEATE YOU OR KILL YOU.

TRADITIONAL

GET ME SOME COFFEE OR I'LL SLAY YOUR ENTIRE FAMILY.

SELF-DEPRECATING

I AM UNWORTHY TO BREATHE THE AIR YOU HAVE BURPED.

CHEERLEADER

OKAY EVERYBODY, LET'S FORM A HUMAN PYRAMID!!

MANAGEMENT STYLES (CONTINUED)

AND MORE...

READ TOO MANY BOOKS

LET'S KEEP SEARCHING FOR EXCELLENCE IN THE QUALITY CHAOS... OR WHATEVER THE JAPANESE ARE DOING THIS MONTH.

DO IT YOURSELF

MAKE UP SOME OBJECTIVES AND GIVE YOURSELF A PERFORMANCE REVIEW... BE OBJECTIVE.

ABSENTEE

I'M OFF AGAIN TO DO INCREDIBLY IMPORTANT THINGS WHERE YOU CAN'T EASILY FIND ME.

S. Adams

INSTRUCTIONS FROM THE BOSS

YOUR BOSS IS A BUSY PERSON WHO CANNOT WASTE TIME CLARIFYING SIMPLE INSTRUCTIONS. YOU HAVE TO USE YOUR OWN BEST JUDGMENT.

CAN ANYBODY READ THE BOSS'S HAND-WRITING? THIS NOTE IS INCOMPREHENSIBLE.

HMM... YES, I THINK IT SAYS "THE CLIENTS MUST BE KILLED AT ONCE."

MAN, I GET ALL THE BAD ASSIGNMENTS.

OR IT COULD HAVE SAID "...BILLED AT ONCE."

YOUR BOSS WILL SPEAK A LANGUAGE THAT IS RELATIVELY EASY TO LEARN, ONCE YOU RECOGNIZE THE PATTERN.

BLAH BLAH BLAH BLAH BLAH

EMPLOYEES ARE OUR MOST IMPORTANT ASSET.

MEANING: NOTHING

OUR STRATEGY IS TO IMPROVE LONG TERM PROFITABILITY.

MEANING: NOTHING

WE ARE STUDYING THAT IMPORTANT ISSUE SO WE CAN PREPARE AN APPROPRIATE ACTION PLAN.

MEANING: NOTHING

THE BIGGER THE BUILD-UP, THE WORSE THE ASSIGNMENT

THE MORE TIME YOUR BOSS SPENDS DESCRIBING YOUR NEXT ASSIGNMENT, THE STUPIDER IT PROBABLY IS.

ANGELS WILL SING YOUR NAME... THE ENTIRE FABRIC OF EXISTENCE WILL DEPEND ON YOUR SUCCESS !!

WOW! ANGELS? REALLY?!

I HAD NO IDEA THAT SCRAPING GUM OFF THE BOTTOMS OF DESKS WAS SO IMPORTANT.

BOSSES NEVER UNDERSTAND WHY THEIR STAFF IS RELUCTANT TO WARN THEM ABOUT PROBLEMS UNTIL IT'S TOO LATE.

THE PROJECT MIGHT NOT BE AS EASY AS WE HOPED.

WHAT?!!

YOU IDIOT!! I'LL FIRE YOU AND ANYBODY WHO LOOKS LIKE YOU!!

WHY DON'T THEY COME TO ME SOONER?

READING BODY LANGUAGE

YOU CAN TELL WHAT
YOUR BOSS IS THINKING
BY LEARNING TO READ
THE SUBTLE, UNCONSCIOUS
SIGNALS OF HIS/HER
BODY.

THIS POSITION SAYS
"I AM NOT OPEN TO
YOUR SUGGESTION."

THIS POSITION SAYS
"I AM NOT LISTENING
TO YOUR SUGGESTION."

THIS POSITION SAYS
"YOU HAVE REPEATED
YOUR SUGGESTION TOO
MANY TIMES."

PERFORMANCE APPRAISALS

IF A MIRACLE OCCURS AND YOUR BOSS ACTUALLY COMPLETES YOUR PERFORMANCE APPRAISAL, IT WILL BE HASTILY PREPARED, ANNOYINGLY VAGUE, AND AN INSULT TO WHATEVER DIGNITY YOU MIGHT STILL POSSESS.

CO-WORKERS

SUFFERING FOOLS

THE WORLD IS FULL OF ATTRACTIVE PEOPLE WHOM YOU WILL NEVER MEET. YOUR ONLY HOPE FOR ROMANCE IS TO LOWER YOUR STANDARDS UNTIL CO-WORKERS LOOK GOOD.

YOU KNOW, WHEN I STARTED HERE, I THOUGHT YOU WERE A COMPLETE LOSER.

BUT NOW I ONLY THINK YOU'RE A SEVEN-EIGHTHS LOSER.

WHEN SHE GETS DOWN TO FIVE-EIGHTHS I'LL MAKE MY MOVE.

THE BOSS'S SECRETARY

THE MOST PERILOUS CHALLENGE YOU
WILL EVER FACE IS DEALING WITH
THE BOSS'S SECRETARY. IT MAY BE
NECESSARY TO OFFER A LIVE CALF
OR A SUMMER INTERN AS AN
ANIMAL SACRIFICE.

UNDERSTANDING ACCOUNTING PEOPLE

PEOPLE WHO WORK IN ACCOUNTING DEPARTMENTS OFTEN WORK TWELVE-HOUR DAYS CREATING REPORTS THAT NOBODY CARES ABOUT. THIS GIVES THEM A VERY BAD ATTITUDE. DO NOT ATTEMPT HUMOR AROUND THEM.

ARE YOU THE CLERK WHO RETAINS ALL OF THE BUDGET ANALYSIS RECORDS?

WHAT IF I AM?

THEN I GUESS YOU COULD BE CONSIDERED "ANALYSIS RETENTIVE."

Hee Hee

HE WAS MIGHTY FAST WITH THOSE SCISSORS.

UNDERSTANDING TECHNICAL PEOPLE

TECHNICAL PEOPLE
RESPOND TO QUESTIONS
IN THREE WAYS.

IT IS TECHNICALLY
IMPOSSIBLE.

MEANING: I DON'T FEEL LIKE
DOING IT.

IT DEPENDS...

MEANING: ABANDON ALL HOPE OF
A USEFUL ANSWER.

THE DATA BITS ARE FLEXED
THROUGH A COLLECTIMIZER
WHICH STRIPS THE FLOW-
GATE ARRAYS INTO VIRTUAL
MESSAGE ELEMENTS...

MEANING: I DON'T KNOW.

S. Adams

MARKETING

TRANSLATING MARKETING TALK

PEOPLE IN MARKETING JOBS ALWAYS SPEAK IN CODE.

OOWA OOWAGA

WE DID EXHAUSTIVE CUSTOMER RESEARCH.

MEANING: I ASKED MY CAT, MITTENS.

I'M SURE WE CAN SELL A MILLION UNITS.

MEANING: YEAH, RIGHT, WHEN PIGS FLOSS.

WE'RE WORKING CLOSELY WITH THE ENGINEERS.

MEANING: WE TOLD THEM OUR FAVORITE COLORS.

UNDERSTANDING MARKETING PEOPLE

PEOPLE ENTER THE MARKETING PROFESSION AFTER THEY REALIZE THAT THEY HAVE GROWN UP WITHOUT ANY PARTICULAR SKILLS.

PERKS

BUSINESS LUNCHES

WHEN USING THE COMPANY'S MONEY
TO PAY FOR A MEAL, IT IS EXPECTED
THAT YOU WILL ORDER THE MOST
EXPENSIVE ITEMS ON THE MENU.

STEALING OFFICE SUPPLIES

SICK DAYS

SICK DAYS ARE THE SAME
AS VACATION DAYS, BUT
WITH SOUND EFFECTS.

THE JOY OF FEEDBACK

FEEDBACK IS A BUSINESS TERM WHICH REFERS TO THE JOY OF CRITICIZING OTHER PEOPLE'S WORK. THIS IS ONE OF THE FEW GENUINE PLEASURES OF THE JOB, AND YOU SHOULD MILK IT FOR ALL IT'S WORTH.

LEGAL OWNERSHIP OF YOUR PEN ENDS WHEN YOU TAKE YOUR EYES OFF OF IT. YOUR CO-WORKERS ARE WAITING FOR ANY OPPORTUNITY TO MAKE IT THEIR OWN.

MEETINGS

USING STEREOTYPES TO SIZE UP A MEETING

YOU CAN USE STEREOTYPES TO RAPIDLY DETERMINE WHO HAS THE MOST POWER AT A BUSINESS MEETING.

RETURNING CALLS DURING A MEETING: MUST BE A MIDDLE MANAGER.

BROUGHT A BAG LUNCH: MUST BE A TECHNICAL PERSON.

HAS NO WRITING MATERIALS: MUST BE A SENIOR EXECUTIVE.

UNAWARE THAT VESTS ARE NOT IN STYLE: MUST BE A BUDGET ANALYST.

TOO MUCH MAKE-UP AND CLEAVAGE: SECRETARY WHO MAY BE HAVING AN AFFAIR WITH AN EXECUTIVE.

TRYING TO LOOK MORE RELAXED THAN ANYBODY ELSE: PROBABLY AN EXECUTIVE.

THE IMPORTANCE OF DONUTS

NEVER CALL A MEETING BEFORE NOON WITHOUT DONUTS OR ALL ORDER WILL BE LOST.

DOGBERT'S GROUP I.Q. FORMULA

THE INTELLIGENCE QUOTIENT OF ANY MEETING CAN BE DETERMINED BY STARTING WITH 100 AND SUBTRACTING 5 POINTS FOR EACH PARTICIPANT.

DEALING WITH MEETING BOREDOM

YOU CAN ACTUALLY DIE FROM THE BOREDOM CAUSED BY LONG BUSINESS MEETINGS. THERE ARE THREE BASIC STRATEGIES FOR SURVIVAL:

FANTASIZE

CRACK JOKES

IS THAT YOUR NOSE OR DID A WEASEL CLIMB ON YOUR FACE AND DIE?

GO FOR IT

USING MEETINGS TO AVOID WORK

DOGBERT'S RULE OF THREE

NOTHING PRODUCTIVE EVER HAPPENS
WITH MORE THAN THREE PEOPLE IN
A ROOM, BECAUSE SOMEBODY IS
ALWAYS TOO DISTRACTED TO
PARTICIPATE IN A MEANINGFUL WAY.

FRIDAY AFTERNOON MEETINGS

CALENDAR MULTIPLIER EFFECT

IT IS FUTILE TO TRY TO ARRANGE A MEETING WITH MORE THAN THREE PARTICIPANTS. BEYOND THREE IT IS STATISTICALLY IMPOSSIBLE TO FIND A DATE WHEN ALL OF YOU WILL BE AVAILABLE.

THE DILBERT DRONE

THE MOST EFFECTIVE WAY TO RESPOND TO A QUESTION IS TO DRONE ENDLESSLY ABOUT UNRELATED TOPICS. THIS HAS THE DUAL ADVANTAGE OF AVOIDING GIVING WRONG ANSWERS AND REDUCING THE VOLUME OF FUTURE QUESTIONS.

WEASEL WORDS, BLUFFING, AND LYING

PRESENTING BAD NEWS

WEASEL WORDS ARE WORDS THAT ARE TRUE WITHOUT BEING INFORMATIVE. THEY ARE USEFUL IN SITUATIONS WHERE A CLEAR EXPLANATION WOULD BE EMBARRASSING.

THE VALUE OF BUZZWORDS

DOGBERT'S RULE OF BUSINESS LIES

SALESMEN

SALESMEN ARE ALWAYS ANXIOUS TO DEFINE THEMSELVES AS YOUR PARTNER, PART OF YOUR TEAM; IN FACT, ANYTHING BUT THE MONEY-SUCKING-BRIEFCASE-TOTING-LEECHES THAT THEY ARE.

I'M NOT JUST A SALESMAN ... I'M PART OF YOUR TEAM!

AND I'LL BE HAPPY TO HOLD ONTO "OUR" MONEY FOR US.

LYING ON YOUR RÉSUMÉ

NOBODY EVER GOT A JOB BY BEING COMPLETELY HONEST ON THEIR RÉSUMÉ. MAKE YOUR LIES BOLD, CREATIVE, AND ABOVE ALL: UNVERIFIABLE.

YOUR RÉSUMÉ SHOWS TWENTY YEARS AS A SENIOR EXECUTIVE AT THE CIA...

YES, AND THEY ARE INSTRUCTED TO KILL ANYBODY WHO TRIES TO CHECK ON IT.

EXCUSES FOR BEING LATE

NOBODY KNOWS ANY MORE THAN YOU DO

PEOPLE WHO SOUND SMART ARE USUALLY BLUFFING. YOU CAN UNCOVER THEIR BLUFFS BY USING SIMPLE INTERROGATION.

IT'S A LOT LIKE THE WIGMAN LEAST SQUARES INVENTORY METHOD.

COULD YOU EXPLAIN THAT METHOD RIGHT NOW?

AH, YES, WELL, YOU GOT YOUR INVENTORY, RIGHT? THEN YOU DO SOME MATH AND... HEY, IS THAT MY PHONE RINGING?

S. Adams

TECHNOLOGY AND INNOVATION

INNOVATION

COMPANIES ARE GENERALLY SLOW TO
ADOPT NEW WAYS OF BUSINESS,
ESPECIALLY IF IT MEANS A REDUCTION
IN THEIR BELOVED PAPER.

HOW TECHNOLOGY FREES US FROM WORK

TELECOMMUTE YOUR WAY TO MORE LEISURE TIME

FOR ONE BRIEF TECHNOLOGICAL WINDOW IN HISTORY, IT IS POSSIBLE TO CLAIM YOU ARE WORKING AT HOME BUT NEARLY IMPOSSIBLE FOR YOUR BOSS TO CHECK ON YOU. YOU SHOULD ARRANGE FOR AT LEAST ONE TELECOMMUTE DAY PER WEEK.

LIE TO YOUR COMPUTER

COMPUTERS HATE PEOPLE. THEY WILL DESTROY YOUR DATA JUST TO BE MEAN. YOUR BEST STRATEGY IS TO LIE TO YOUR COMPUTER AND CONVINCE IT THAT YOU DON'T CARE ABOUT YOUR DATA.

ALL PROGRESS IS BASED ON FAULTY ASSUMPTIONS

NOBODY WOULD TRY ANYTHING NEW IF THEY UNDERSTOOD THE CONSEQUENCES. THEREFORE, ALL PROGRESS IS BASED ON FAULTY ASSUMPTIONS.

DOGBERT

EXAMPLE #1

I CALL IT THE "WHEEL" AND IT WILL MAKE CIVILIZATION MUCH LESS COMPLICATED.

REALLY?

EXAMPLE #2

I CALL IT THE "TELEVISION," AND IT WILL BE A BOON TO CULTURE AND EDUCATION.

REALLY?

EXAMPLE #3

I CALL IT A "PERSONAL COMPUTER," AND IT WILL ELIMINATE PAPER WHILE FREEING US ALL FROM TEDIOUS AND UNFULFILLING JOBS.

REALLY?

S. Adams

STYLE VERSUS SUBSTANCE

GREAT IDEAS CAN BE WRITTEN ON GARBAGE

THROUGHOUT HISTORY, MANY GREAT IDEAS STARTED AS SCRIBBLES ON THE BACKS OF ENVELOPES, MATCH BOOKS, AND COCKTAIL NAPKINS. BUT UNLESS YOU'RE PRETTY CONFIDENT ABOUT YOUR IDEA IT IS BEST TO USE REGULAR PAPER WHEN YOU SHOW IT TO THE BOSS.

THIS IS IT? THIS IS YOUR PROPOSAL?

YES SIR, WRITTEN ON THE CORN FLAKES I WAS HAVING WHEN THE IDEA CAME TO ME.

I PROBABLY SHOULDN'T HAVE STAPLED THE PAGES TOGETHER.

THE POWER OF FORMATTING

A WELL-FORMATTED, STUPID PROPOSAL WILL GET FARTHER THAN A GOOD IDEA WHICH IS POORLY FORMATTED.

AT FIRST, I THOUGHT YOUR PROPOSAL WAS RIDICULOUS...

THEN I NOTICED HOW WELL-FORMATTED IT IS, YOUR CREATIVE USE OF ITALICS, THE HIGH QUALITY OF THE PLASTIC COVER... I MUST SAY IT SWAYED ME.

WAIT... WHAT'S THIS LITTLE TWO-DOTTED THING?

IT'S A COLON, SIR. THEY'RE ALL THE RAGE.

S.Adams

ANALYSIS AS A TOOL TO AVOID DECISIONS

THE PURPOSE OF ANALYSIS IS TO AVOID MAKING HARD DECISIONS. THEREFORE, THERE CAN NEVER BE TOO MUCH ANALYSIS.

DID YOU DO A PRESENT VALUE ANALYSIS?

YES.

ENVIRONMENTAL STUDY?

YES

BUDGET ANALYSIS?

YES

STOCKHOLDER IMPACT?

YES

CARBON DATING?

UH...NO

WELL, THEN YOU'RE WASTING MY TIME, AREN'T YOU.

GETTING AWAY WITH IT

GETTING OTHERS TO DO YOUR WORK

THE DOGBERT DEFLECTION

WHEN ASKED A QUESTION, NEVER ADMIT THAT YOU DON'T HAVE THE ANSWER. INSTEAD, RESPOND WITH AN IMPOSSIBLE QUESTION OF YOUR OWN.

DOGBERT, DO YOU HAVE THE MONTHLY SALES TOTALS FOR THE BOSS?

YES, OF COURSE. DO YOU WANT IT BY INDUSTRY CODE, ZIP CODE, PRODUCT CODE, GOOMBA CODE, PENAL CODE OR BLAH BLAH CODE?

UH... I DON'T KNOW...

IF YOU DON'T KNOW WHAT YOU NEED, WHY ARE YOU HERE?

THE BEST WAY TO AVOID CRITICISM IS TO ESTABLISH A REPUTATION FOR BEING IRRATIONAL AND BELLIGERENT AT THE SLIGHTEST EXCUSE.

YOUR REPORT IS ALMOST PERFECT.

ALMOST ??!

YOU'RE PREDJUDICED AGAINST DOGS, YOU BIGOT!! I KNOW YOUR TYPE... ALL SMILES, BUT SECRETLY A DOG HATER. I'VE GOT A LAWYER!!

OKAY, IT'S PERFECT, EXTRAORDINARY, INCREDIBLE.

REALLY, OR ARE YOU JUST SAYING THAT?

S. Adams

HANDLING QUESTIONS

GETTING FIRED

BIG COMPANIES HAVE PROCEDURES THAT MAKE IT NEARLY IMPOSSIBLE TO FIRE ANYBODY. IF YOU HAVE NO CAREER AMBITION AND NO PRIDE YOU CAN TAKE GREAT ADVANTAGE OF THIS SITUATION.

PRIORITIZING YOUR WORK

YOU CAN TELL HOW IMPORTANT AN ASSIGNMENT IS BY HOW IT IS COMMUNICATED TO YOU.

IN BASKET:
TOTALLY UNIMPORTANT. YOU MAY SAFELY IGNORE IT FOREVER.

TELEPHONE:
IGNORE IT. NO IMPORTANT ASSIGNMENT HAS EVER BEEN GIVEN OVER THE TELEPHONE.

RRRRING

PERSONAL THREAT:
MAKE SOME TIME ON YOUR CALENDAR.

TUESDAY?

S. Adams

DOGMAS

DOGBERT'S THEORY OF DELEGATION

ALL ASSIGNMENTS ARE EVENTUALLY DELEGATED TO THE PERSON WHO UNDERSTANDS THEM THE LEAST.

THE IMPORTANCE OF STRATEGIES

ALL COMPANIES NEED A STRATEGY SO THE EMPLOYEES WILL KNOW WHAT THEY DON'T DO.

COMPANY WITH NO STRATEGY

UH-OH...WHAT SHOULD I DO?

RRRRING

COMPANY WITH A STRATEGY

WE DON'T DO THAT.

PESSIMISM AND JOB EXPERIENCE

AN OPTIMIST IS SIMPLY A PESSIMIST WITH NO JOB EXPERIENCE. PESSIMISM INCREASES STEADILY OVER A CAREER UNTIL THE TENTH YEAR AND THEN REMAINS CONSTANT.

JUST HIRED

GREAT IDEA! LET'S START RIGHT AWAY!

FIVE YEARS EXPERIENCE

WE TRIED THAT IDEA FIVE YEARS AGO. IT DIDN'T WORK THEN AND IT WON'T WORK NOW.

TEN YEARS EXPERIENCE

WE'RE ALL GOING TO DIE ... DIE OR GO TO JAIL ... IT'S THE END OF LIFE AS WE KNOW IT ...

THE RIGHT APPROACH

THE CORRECT APPROACH TO ANY SITUATION IS, BY AMAZING COINCIDENCE, THE ONLY APPROACH YOU KNOW.

THIS IS A CLASSIC APPLICATION FOR THE "SWANSON WEIGHTED CASH FLOW ANALYSIS," WHICH I KNOW SO WELL.

NO, NO, WE NEED TO BUILD A COMPUTER MODEL.

BAH! WE JUST NEED TO KICK SOME HINEYS, THAT'S ALL.

LISTEN TO ME, PEOPLE! WE MUST STICK THEM WITH QUILLS – IT'S THE ONLY WAY!

EVOLUTION OF A FACT

WILD GUESSES CAN BE TRANSFORMED INTO BUSINESS FACTS THROUGH THE MIRACLE OF COMMUNICATIONS.

STEP ONE: WILD GUESS

I DUNNO... IT COULD BE ANYWHERE FROM ONE TO A MILLION.

STEP TWO: RUMOR

THEY SAY IT COULD BE A MILLION.

STEP THREE: FACT

EXPERTS SAY ONE MILLION.

RUMORS

ALL RUMORS ARE TRUE – ESPECIALLY IF YOUR BOSS DENIES THEM.

I HEARD THAT WE'RE ALL GOING TO BE RECLASSIFIED AS "SERFS."

AND THEY'LL MAKE US WEAR PAPER HATS.

...AND WE'LL HAVE TO SALUTE ANYBODY FROM THE MARKETING DEPARTMENT!

THE LOBOTOMIES ARE SCHEDULED FOR TUESDAY!

THESE RUMORS ARE RIDICULOUS. WE ARE <u>NOT</u> CONSIDERING LOBOTOMIES...

CERTAINLY NOT AT THE PRICES WE WERE QUOTED.

DOGBERT'S RULE OF STRATEGIES

ANY GOOD STRATEGY WILL SEEM RIDICULOUS BY THE TIME IT IS IMPLEMENTED.

EXECUTIVE OFFICES

LET'S OFFER AN EARLY RETIREMENT INCENTIVE.

YEAH, THAT WAY WE CAN AVOID LAYOFFS.

THE EMPLOYEES WILL UNDERSTAND AND LOVE US.

LOWER MANAGEMENT

WE HAVE TO ROUND UP THE EXPERIENCED EMPLOYEES AND PAY THEM TO LEAVE.

WHAT YOU DO

HOW TO IDENTIFY AN EXPERT

AN EXPERT IS A PERSON WHO HAS BEEN ASSIGNED TO AN EXPERT'S JOB. NO OTHER QUALIFICATIONS ARE NECESSARY.

EXPERT

NON-EXPERT

DUHH...

EXPERT

GO AHEAD, ASK ME ANYTHING.

BUSINESS CARD

DOGBERT'S TIPS

HOW TO MAKE YOUR BORING JOB SOUND DANGEROUS

EVEN THE MOST MUNDANE BUSINESS ACTIVITIES CAN SOUND GLORIOUS IF YOU DESCRIBE THEM IN ANGRY AND VIOLENT TERMS. BUT REMEMBER TO SPEAK METAPHORICALLY, OR IT WILL SOUND SILLY.

CORRECT

I'VE BEEN PUTTING OUT FIRES ALL DAY!

SO I SAID "DON'T SHOOT THE MESSENGER!"

ALSO CORRECT

IT'S A BOMB WAITING TO GO OFF!

MAYBE I'LL DODGE A BULLET THIS TIME!

I'LL HAVE TO FALL ON MY SWORD IF THIS DOESN'T WORK!

INCORRECT

I WROTE A MEMO AND WENT TO LUNCH!

WHEN TO CHANGE JOBS

CHANGING JOBS IS A TRAUMATIC AND DEGRADING PROCESS. YOU SHOULD ONLY DO IT WHEN YOUR CURRENT JOB BECOMES UNBEARABLE. FIND YOURSELF ON THIS GUIDE TO HELP YOUR DECISION.

KEEPING YOUR PERSPECTIVE

YOUR JOB IS UTTERLY INSIGNIF-
ICANT. BUT ON THE PLUS SIDE,
NOTHING YOU COULD DO WOULD
SERIOUSLY DAMAGE THE PLANET.
DON'T TAKE ANY OF IT TOO
SERIOUSLY.

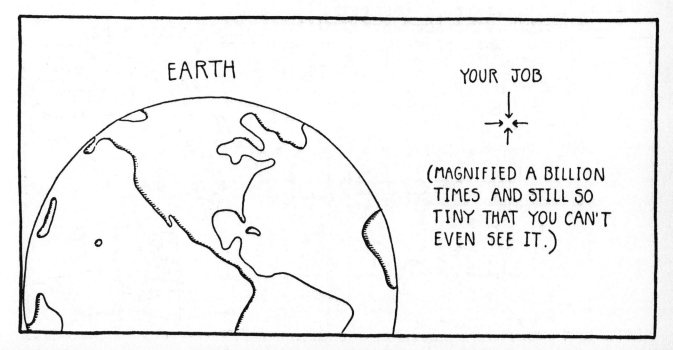

EARTH

YOUR JOB

(MAGNIFIED A BILLION
TIMES AND STILL SO
TINY THAT YOU CAN'T
EVEN SEE IT.)

FUNNY BUSINESS

You want to stay ahead of the competition, right? Of course right! Then your next job is to acquire these other high quality, low-cost 𝑛𝑏 titles. ...

CLUES FOR THE CLUELESS
Dogbert's Big Book of Manners
Illustrated by Scott Adams £4.99
'Of course, you could buy some other book on etiquette, and in it you might find such useful titbits as what kind of uniform the upstairs servants should wear, or the proper way to address the Pope when you meet him in person. But if you want practical information – like what to do after you sneeze in your hand – then you have to buy this book. It's the only book that speaks to you as the unwashed heathen that you know you are.' DOGBERT
Alternatively titled Sleeves Make Elegant Napkins and They Always Match Your Outfit, this time the little dog has a bone to pick with us about our appalling post-modern manners.

BUILD A BETTER LIFE BY STEALING OFFICE SUPPLIES
Dogbert's Big Book of Business
Illustrated by Scott Adams £4.99
Dogbert, the entrepreneurial quadruped from the nationally syndicated DILBERT® strip, expounds on the dog-eat-dog world of work.

—————— **Total Books**

Yes, please rush me the above books. My cheque or money order for _____ is enclosed!
(Please add £2.95 per book for postage and handling. Make cheque or money order payable to Nicholas Brealey Publishing Ltd.)

Name _____

Address _____

City _____ Post Code _____

Return to Nicholas Brealey Publishing Ltd, 36 John Street, London WC1N 2AT or phone +44 (0)171 430 0224 or fax +44 (0)171 404 8311 for Credit Card Sales.